THE
GODS
R
WATCHING

GW00702960

A poetry collection

Dale Brendan Hyde (c)

Verso page

ISBN: 978-1-912543-18-2

THE AUTHOR. DALE BRENDAN HYDE was born in Salford in 1974, yet has lived most of his life in the City of Wakefield West Yorkshire. A troubled life throughout his teens, seen a crescendo into a lengthy prison sentence for robbery, where upon release a mixture of attending college to retake failed schooling & continued trouble with the police & high courts seemed to be his course in life, until a university place seemingly became the catalyst to a more determined path of making his occupation that of a Writer. He published his first poetry book by Route at the Yorkshire Art circus for the TS Elliot prize. Contributions to other writers books followed & magazine articles on his passion of bare knuckle boxing reveal his extensive repertoire in his writing styles. Trouble free now for over a decade, his debut novel THE INK RUN finally showed the true depth of his talent. His first short story, titled, The Whiskey Pool is available on Amazon kindle. He is currently over half way through his second crime fiction novel, titled, The Death Row Thrift Shop, which will be released early spring 2019.

Chapter sequence

WHO KNOWS WHERE YOU SHALL LAY

ON THE DUSTY & SWEPT SHELVES

NEAR TO HUXLEY & HORACE

NEAR A MISPLACED BEHAN'S SURPRISE

A THOUSAND YEARS WE LAY

SIDE BY SIDE

LONG BEFORE OUR BONES

TROD THIS LITERARY WORLD

OUR INK PENS

WITH CRAMPED WRISTS

TWIRLED INTO THE NIGHT

AT LAST HER EYES

MATCHED THE FULL MOON

BRIGHT & UP THERE

RESEMBLANCE MEANT SALVATION

OUR LIVES I FELT

COULD AT LAST START AGAIN

MAYBE THE MAN IN THE MOON

HAD DONE WITH US

STRIPPED US FINALLY

THIS TIME OF MADNESS

HER EYES WERE SO BEAUTIFUL

& CLEAR

LIKE A PLANET

OUT IN THE FUTURE

THERE'S MURDER

INSIDE THE GOLD MINE

SPARKS OF DIAMOND RICOCHETS

COPPER COLOURED SMELLS OF

DEATH TRICKLED SILVER FLAKES

BELOW THE EARTHS

NEW BURIED BONES

GREED SEE'S LIFE FADE AGAIN

WE ARE BIGGER THAN MARS

FIT TEN PLUTO'S DOWN HERE

CLOSER THAN US TO THE SUN

SMALLER STILL

PLACED THE MERCURY ONE

WE SIT IN LINE NEXT TO VENUS

THE RING BACK

WE WANT FROM SATURN

SO NEPTUNE ONLY SHADED

URANUS LIGHTER BLUE'S

5

SPARE CHANGE

SOME BEADS

FOR YOUR SWEETHEART

FOR MINE

THE HEAT OF

HURRICANE WINDS FLYING BY

A COOL CARIB IN CHRISTCHURCH

QUENCHING THIRST

SHANTY TOWN RUM SHACKS

DRIPPING TO BURST

BY NIGHT

LET THE OCEAN VERSE

DIP THE ROUGH ATLANTIC

FALL & CRASH LIKE REGGAE DRUMS

TOURISTIC VIBE REHEARSED

OTHER SIDE FALLS SMOOTHER

DISTANT HUMS & FIGHTS

FLASH OF FISHER BOATS

TWINKLE AS RETIRING RED SUN SEE'S

DESERTED BEACHES

NEW LOVERS IN THE SANDS

FOOTSTEPS WASHED OUT OF SIGHT

UNKNOWN REGGAE LANDS

WALKED THE HOT DAY

HAND IN HAND

BY THE PALMS

SWAYING LIKE CROP OUT

MIGHTY BARBADIAN

DRUMS OUT

6

All I ever really hear

From the blacks of this earth

How we the whites repressed them

Since slavery birth

Slaves I never agreed with

People are the same

Blacks are just as racist

So who the Hell's to blame

Forgiveness I am ready

For the insults of a past

Generations tuned into greed

For money that never lasts

This centuries rappers

Will try a snidey blast

Spitting words to put me down

Yes I reflect white

So how can I forget all

The harshness of my past

Media black hip hoppers

Try to cast

Glances from an eye

To a pupil harassed

We have ghettoes

Whites know that

So if you really

Want to unite

Like dogs should to cats

Less talk about

All the racist

Chit chat

What when funeral

Flowers fade

Is this the time

To move on

I think not

Hanging sad in

Old vases

My head hangs

In pain

Yet I notice his

fighting shadow

and smile for

your life again

THE WILD RIVER OF DEATH

COMES FLOODING BACK

FLASH OF OLD ENEMIES

THE RUSH OF AN ATTACK

ANTAGONISTIC NATURE OF THE
UNKNOWN SCREAM

NEVER SOUNDED LIKE GUNFIRE

TO A NOW DEAFENED EAR

MORE LIKE A HUNTING HORN

AS I CHASED THOSE MEN

WITH FEAR

FLOOR ONE MASS BLACK

AND WHITE CHESSBOARD

CRIPPLED PRISONERS

OF WAR

SMALL POWERLESS PAWNS

WHILE THE MIGHTY QUEEN

STANDS LIKE DEATH AT THE BACK

IMAGES BRANDED INTO MY MIND

CAPTURED DEATH CAMP MEMBERS

STILL AND COLD

WET AND FILTHY

ALL SO DEAD

SOMETIMES MY RIFLE SIGHTS

MY PARANOID VISION

TRAINED ON THE ENEMY

FOR CONFUSED FUN AND TORMENT

HAUNTING THE WORLD WITH THIS
GHOST

I DROP SO EASY

SO SAD

MARCHED ON ALL THROUGH

THE WEARY NIGHT

FOR DAYS WE TRUDGED ON

WITH FORLORN HOPE

EVEN MADE SOME BEDS

WITH THE LUCKY DEAD

USELESS FUCKING MEDALS

THE VERY PLACE THEY

NOW FIND THAT THERE PINNED

PAINFUL SHRAPNEL

COULD HAVE BEEN DEFLECTED

CATCH A GLIMPSE

THROUGH THE STINGING TEARS

INSCRIPTIONS ETCHED THERE

LISTENING NOW AGAIN TO

WIND THAT WHISTLES

THROUGH THE BARS

FLICKERS OF MY

RATIONED CANDLE

LEVELS IN WAX

WHERE I HAVE BLOWN IT OUT

REMINDERS OF THE LONG NIGHTS

OF PAIN

TODAY AND TOMORROW

THE HOPE LIES DEAD

EVEN NOW THE NIGHT

BRINGING FLASHES

TO MY MIND

SHARPER AND BRIGHTER

THAN THE JUNGLES I

LIT UP WITH HATRED

DEATH DID SEND

MANY A MESSENGER

THESE DECAYING WARDS

NO COMFORT BROUGHT TO

MY SWEATY FEVERED HEAD

HIGH ABOVE RUSTIC FAN

MESMERISED ME WITH

ITS LAZY REVOLVE

NOTHING FRESH

JUST MORE DANK

STALE AIR

DOCTORS IN DISGUISE

RENDEZVOUS WITH DEATH

BREATHLESS HUSH IN

CORRIDORS TONIGHT

MORE BEDS LAY NOW EMPTY

THE AFTERNOONS DEAD

ALWAYS FILLED WITH

THE WAILING WOUNDED

CRUMPLED SHEETS NOW RED THAT

USE TO FOLD CLEAN AND WHITE

RECOLLECTIONS OF MY

BEAUTIFUL GARDEN BACK HOME

WHEN WINTER COMES

MY FLOWERS FADE

LIKE THE BRAVE MEN

WHO LEAVE TRENCHES AND RUN

HAPPINESS WOULD HAVE BEEN

LOSS OF AMMUNITION

ECSTASY FOR MY IMAGINATION

UNKNOWN SHAPES

LAYING AT MY

EARTH CLOD DEN FEET

OH DEATH

SWEET DEATH

WHY DID YOU LEAVE

ME BE

A

Cool

Run

Of

Sins

Turned

Into

Creation

AT LEAST WHEN

A POOR WRETCH

IS LOVED

HE CAN BE CERTAIN

IT'S SENT FROM ABOVE

DIAMONDS NOW SPARKLE

IN SUCH LOVING STARE

RUBY RED LIPS KISSING

ANSWERED PRAYER

I'M NAMED AFTER

IRISH SAINTS SO RARE

THE EASTER UPRISING

WOULD BE LIKE MY DESPAIR

IN MY LIFE

IF YOU

WERE NO LONGER THERE

11

IF ONLY I

COULD PIN IT

DOWN

GUARANTEE OF

NO MORE

HARM

PROMISES LONG FORGOTTEN

LAYING

DUSTY AND FORLORN

SLEEPING THROUGH

TILL DAWN

LAZING LIKE

SLOWLY SWAYING SUMMER CORN

HORNETS

IT WAS GUESSED

FLYING BLINDLY INTO MY

WEATHER BEATEN NETS

DRIFTER AROUND THIS CITY

SAW A RARE

GIRL SITTING PRETTY

WONDERED IF I

SHOULD WAIT

THE BLUE BUS

SHOULD COME SOON

MY FARE CAUGHT

A GLARE TO MY EYE

AS IT

ROLLED AWAY TOWARDS

THE SUNNY GUTTER

FACES NOW

PASSING BY ME

VOICES

SOUNDING LIKE MUTTERS

PASSED A HOUSE

WHERE THE DOOR

WAS THE COLOR OF HEAVEN

WINDOWS LOOKED LIKE ANGELS

INVITING THE CROWDS

CURTAINS

HANGING CASUAL

LIKE ALLURING SILVER SHROUDS

I LIKE THE WAY

PICASSO FLOWS

MIXED IN BLACK AND WHITE

LIKE TWO

SIDES OF MY MIND

DISTRACTION FROM

PEN

I NOTICE BRASS DAGGER

CLOSE BY

FAVOURITE FINGERED

FICTION

LAYS WITHOUT DUST

TO LEARN TO GET BY

OWN STYLE

NEVER MISTAKE THAT ONE

EVEN THOUGH ITS

NEW

HOW DID IT BECOME

ADVISE IF YOU

CHECK BETWEEN

THE LINES

LEARNED THE HARD WAY

BETTER SAY THAT

WHICKER BASKET

FULL OF VERSE

MAYBE EVEN THIS

ONE SHOULD HAVE

BEEN BURNT

SPECIAL BINDER

SECURING HOPEFULL

FUTURE

TRIED MANY THINGS

SEEMS

THIS IS MY CURE

CERTAIN PARTNER

ENABLES DOUBLE THE LOAD

SCHIZOPHRENIC SIGNATURE

SOMETIMES

ON MY WORK

DATED NEVER

PAPERS

ALL A BLUR

THE DREAMS

YOU HAVE THE

MOMENT

THE GODS I'M TOLD

WATCH US IT SEEMS

LOOK AND SEE

THROUGH

MY WINDOW

BEARING

INTO MY SOUL

LOOK AND SEE ALL

THE TOMMOROW'S

THEY NOW

LAY DEAD AND OLD

IT'S TIME TO SEE THE

PROOF

IT'S THE TIME TO

REVEAL THE TRUTH

IT'S THE TIME NOW

FOR SOME PEACE

SURELY

MY RELEASE

LOOK

AND SEE THROUGH THE

SHADOWS

AT THE DARKENING

GLOOM

LOOK AT ALL THE HOURS

SINCE I'VE BEEN

HOME

IT WONT BE LONG NOW

UNTILL I'M NO LONGER

ALONE

IT'S TIME FOR A

NEW WORLD

IT'S TIME

FOR MY DREAM

HOME WITH YOU MOTHER

JUST LIKE THE

OLD TIMES

USED TO BE

14

COOL CLOAK COLLECTED

BLANKET OF SNOW

CHILLED MOST

TONIGHT

WRAPPED ITSELF AROUND

OUR VILLAGE

LANE

FELL SILENT ORANGE

BY THE STREET

LIGHT

CLIMBED STEADY UPON

MY WINDOW LEDGE TO

STARE

PEOPLE CARRIED ON

WITH ARCTIC

LIVES

STREADILY BUILDING

WHITE CAPS OF

HAIR

THE DAWN OF SUCH A NEW DAY

REPLENISHED THE AWE OF NIGHT

16

SO

YOU SAY

YOU'VE GONE AND DONE

WHAT YOU SAID YOU

WOULD NEVER DO

PUT OUT

A CONTRACT ON

MY SOUL

BUT YOU WILL

NEVER FIND A

KILLER

WILLINGLY THAT COLD

VISIONS LIKE PRISONS

SCARS RUGGED

LIKE THE BARS

GOING NOWHERE FREE

SAYS THE BOSS

SLEPT AND AWOKE

WITH THOUGHTS TO PROVOKE

OH FORGET IT MAN

I SHALL SOBER UP

EMPTY LAYING VESSEL

OR LAST NIGHTS

BROKEN FLOWING CUP

TWISTED METAL

PRECIOUS POLISHED STREAM

GOLDEN BRASS COLOURED

FISH IN THE SEA

FACES AND ROSES

SWEPT OUT OF REACH

ACCOMPANIED BY OTHERS

SAME FICTITIOUS DREAM

*TEMPLES OF MOUNTAINOUS SELDOM
YEARS*

PRESENT POT OF PORCELAIN

PATTERNED SINCERE

ILLUMINATIONS OF THE DARK

SIDE OF THE VEINS

TOO LITTLE TEMPTATION

REVEALS THE OTHER DOMAIN

DESERT LIFE COLOURING OF

THE CONTORTIONIST PLAIN

ENGULFED THE WAXY CANDLES

GHOSTLY BOBBIN FLAME

19

Lead leaves this

Wood surround

My mind starts to

Be explored

Letters become words

Formed to please

A sentence flow

Reveals hidden thoughts

Erased employment

Poised ready at the end

Mistakes rubbed away

If you wish

Unlike life the pencil

Can easily mend

Finger and thumb

Hold the tablet

And chalk

Even more new

Words revealed

Once spoken into talk

Analysis

Your fate is sealed

Unconscious thought

You steal the

Message I leave

Words written

Immortalised

Left on the page a

Thousand years

That's the deal

Benevolent advice

Helping

Soothing

Sure

Every day I write

My thoughts

Keeping my conscience

Pure

20

CRAWLING

NO MORE FEARS LEFT

GRASPING

TOWARDS THE DUSTY DRY EDGE

STOMACH EMPTY

BREAKFAST OVER THE LIP

STONES AND RUBBLE

FALL

EFFORTLESSLY DOWNWARDS

SPIRALLED CHIPPINGS WHIRL

IN THE WIND

DAMAGED BODY

HURTING LIKE DEATH

IS LIFE AT THE CREVICE OR

SPIRITUAL REST

EVEN THE STRONGEST WINE

NEVER SPUN ME THIS WAY

AS I BEGIN THE DESCENT IT

FEELS SURREAL

DISTRESS HITS ME

BEFORE I HIT WITH A MESS

BOTTOM FLOOR CAME FAST

REALIZATION

THERE IS NO GOING BACK

LIFE NEVER FLASHED PAST

IN A MOVIE KINDA WAY

THE DEATH SCENE NOTED

IT'S HUMAN FINAL DAY

THE OTHER SIDE

TRAVELLED SLOW

TO AN UNKNOWN LAND

PLACE WHERE YOU GET CHANCE

TO BOAST

DEVILS GOT TIGHT GRIP

OF YOUR NOW DEADENED HAND

COULDN'T TAKE MY

EYES

FROM HIS SHARP

DIRTY HORNS

IMPALED NOW

I COULD NOT NOTICE

MY ONCE

BEAUTIFUL SIGHT

SCARRED TISSUE LEFT BURNING

IN HELLS FIRE

BRIGHT

Some days you don't feel like writing

Words don't flow how you would like

Some make no sense

So I shall stop now

Or just waste my valuable ink

When your mind is

More powerful

Than the drug

What do you do?

Do you turn towards

the alcohol

Or do you

Try something new

When your mind

Is craving so bad

It can feel

Septic

Do you turn mad?

or do you finally

accept it?

EVEN THOUGH YOUR

ABSENT FROM MY DAY

I MAKE MY JOURNEY ALONG

WINDING LEAFY LANES

FROM MY DOOR WHICH OPENS

UPON EMPTY ORCHARDS

IN THE DISTANCE NOW

I SEE YOUR

FRESHLY DUG GRAVE

CHURCHES SPIRALLED TIP

SKEWERS THE BLACK CLOUDS

THROUGHOUT THE TRIP

ALL YOUR NEW NEIGHBOUR'S TOMBS

ARE CLEAN AND SECURE

SURE IN MY HEART THAT EVEN

UNDERGROUND YOU

MADE MANY FRIENDS ONCE MORE

FRESH ARE YOUR FAVOURITE

FLOWERS

I GRASP THEM GENTLY

IN MY HAND

CARRIED TO YOU AS A GIFT

FROM THE LIVING OLD LAND

MANY RECALLS TO THE MIND

OF OUR MEMORIES MADE

RUSTY VICTORIAN GATES

WITH NO VISIBLE BELL TO ENTER

GREET MY EYES THAT CRY

INSIDE THE FULL YARD

MY SOLID BONES

FEEL A NOW WHIPPING COLD

A CAUTIOUS PATH I TREAD

WITHOUT MUCH CONSCIOUS THOUGHT

I'VE TROD THESE HOP SCOTCH GRAVES

IN A NIGHTMARE

MANY TIMES BEFORE

THREE MAYBE FOUR TIMES A NIGHT

I AWAKE FROM THEM

YOUR DEATH SCENE

SPREADING THROUGH MY MIND

THE HARDNESS NOW OF

YOUR GRAVE PLATE

ENABLES ME TO ROLL

FINISHED TASK I STRIKE WITH A

LAZY HAND

ALWAYS IN CONTROL

HARSH COLD WIND MIXES NOW

WITH MY STONED WORDS

SOME DAYS WHEN I WILL

FEEL BLUE

I WILL CARRY IN A BAG YOU LENT ME

A SPADE

DIG DOWN DEEP

AT LEAST FOUR FEET

TO THE LEVEL WHERE

YOU NOW LAY

JUST NEED TO LET THE DUST THAT WAS

MY BEST FRIEND

SEEP THROUGH MY FINGERS

ONCE AGAIN

ALWAYS ON YOUR DAY

OF BIRTH

I WILL AMBLE UP TO

YOUR MODERN MAUSOLEUM

CAMERA WILL HOLD INSIDE

CHEERFUL RECORD

WHAT SHOULD HAVE BEEN

ALBUM TITLED

LOSS

FULL OF EMPTY VAULTS

INSTEAD OF YOUR

HEAVENLY SMILING FACE

SO SITTING WITH YOUR GRAVE

AS A REST FOR MY BACK

I CONVERSE ON THE GRASS

TELLING YOU ABOUT MY DAY

MELLOW JOINT SOON SCORCHES DOWN

NEEDY LIPS CONSUMED

HALF WAY THOUGH

I HOLD IT UP

HARSH GUSTS OF WIND

ENTWINE DARK CATACOMBS

EVEN THOUGH YOUR

NEVER A WITNESS NO

MORE TO MY LIFE

I ALWAYS LEAVE MY RESPECT

TO AN UNFAIR END

EVEN IN DEATH I WILL NEVER

BOGART YOU MY FRIEND

JUST GOT SO CAUGHT

UP IN THIS WORLD

WHERE ELSE SHOULD I LIVE OUT

THIS GIFT OF LIFE

THE BLOOD PULSATES

THROUGH EVERY HEALTHY VEIN

CONSTANT REMINDERS OF YOUTH

TIMES CHANGE

I NEVER THOUGHT MY TIME

WAS STUCK

EACH SMALL REMINDER

BUILDS THE PICTURE

AS I LAY BACK AND

WONDER WHAT NEW THOUGHTS

SHOULD I LET YOU READ?

WHEN IT BECOMES A TIRING JOB

I PROMISE TO STOP WHEN

IT BECOMES A CHORE

SUCH A FINE PLEASURE

AT THIS MOMENT I FEEL

HOPING ONE DAY FOR

SOMEONE TO READ

ALL BEFORE YOU

LAID OUT ON THE SHEET

JUST AN EQUAL UNDERSTANDING

HOW THIS MIND

OF MINE WORKS

LIVE AND BREATHE YOUR LIFE

MAY GOD HAVE HIS LIBRARY

WRITE YOUR CHAPTER

READ YOUR CENTURY

WORKING MUNDANE

IS NO FUN

BECOME AS THE GREAT TRIBES

LIVE LIFE

THE WAY OF OLD HAS SHOWN

AMONGST GROUPS OF WANDERING
FRIENDS

TO WONDER

YOUR WORDS BEFORE

I will tell you

Where I'm sitting

Still in those prisons

Singing those sad songs

Even though I'm free now

Trapped forever long

Release me false friend

I know you are not that strong

I remember though

The youth of us both

Damn I was bold

Still feel the need to

Climb on the highest court

Roof tops

To shout out the truth

Not being told

God I feel centuries old

Never seen the years

Etch hard on my face

Wondered when I got out

Why innocence had no grace

Still wonder

Where the youth goes

In the prisons

Strange space

WHERE ARE YOU

JIM

NO MORE MOONS LEFT

FOR YOU TO SWIM

SHOW YOURSELF

LIZARD KING

THREE STILL WAITING

FOR THE CALL

OFFICE CRUMBLING

GETTING KINDA OLD

CELEBRATION IF YOU SING

RING RING RING

Sat with chin upon knees

Open window

Collects my thoughts

Within the breeze

High up ledge

Mind now begins to swim

All but one bare tree akin

Branches set for the wind

A runway of the mind

Mighty surge, a single leaf

Clinging onto familiarity

Slow motion, look again

Gathers up now

Along and away

Dancing wind to the free beats

Tree stumped back their

Natural seats

Wind a conductor

Branches clap together

Appreciation

Of such an elegant show

Moon is the spotlight

Sky a vast auditorium

The stars bright sparkles

Are but torches to your seat

Planets would marvel

Powers so strange

Inside bark

Circles of age

Secret notches

Reveal

Stories from our race

A LIGHT ON YOUR EYES

SHOWS THE OCEANS BLUE DIVINE

A MATCH FOR YOUR HAIR

OF SAHARA SANDS I NEED NOT
COMPARE

TRUE RESPONSIVE ARE THOSE LIPS

SO FULL NO PUCKER NEEDS OFFER FOR
KISS

CURVES THAT OFTEN SEEM
SCULPTURED

TO MY WILDEST DREAMS

SWEETNESS IS SUCH YOUR NATURE

CONSUMED BY NOW A NEED

OF YOUR SCENT

I MUST CONFESS TO GREED

A SPRING FLOWER

NO POINT TO COMPARE

FOR THEY FADE BUT ONCE A YEAR

NO WITHER DID I EVER SEE

FROM YOUR LIMBS

STRONG YET GRACED

WITH SOFT TOUCHING SKIN

As I felt my gaze

Pull towards her

She seemed to move

Languidly through the crowd

I watched her curse every

Motionless face

That passed her by

The traffic light on red

Made her move

To the back bumpers

Of stationary cars

The pathway was her enemy

She knew I was watching her

She loved playing to a crowd

However small

31

PEBBLES

POLISHED

COURTESY

OF

THE

SEA'S

Told my girl

I'm a lucky coin

She's a fool

If she ever spends

me

IN THE BREEZE

MY WORRIED POURS

SEND OUT A SCENT

THAT FLOATS ACROSS

THE BEACH

A FISH SHAPED PRINT

BUT THAT'S NOT TO BE BELIEVED

THE KILLER OF MY PARENTS IS NEAR

A THUD RETURNS

FOR ITS STOMACH YEARNS

MY FATE IT SEEMS IS SEALED

THE BAG THEY USED

BLOODIED STILL

SHARP PAINS FOR ME

FOR THEM A THRILL

THE COLD WET SAND

ONCE ONLY MY LAND

SHALL BECOME IT SEEMS

MY EXTINCTION

MY END

Born from within safety

Inside the wet

Protective space

Birth is

The light

Shines on

In a space of time

Your own segment

Your life

A light goes off

Cold earth

Constricts your

Useless vehicle

A body froze

Death is

COMPLETE QUADROPHENIA

MAY BE THE DISEASE

EA TING IT'S

BREAKFAST

AT MY MINDS

TABLE OF DELIGHTS

THE ROTTEN CORE

OF MY CROWN

NOTHING VISIBLE

ON THE SOFT PALLET

A PORTRAYAL OF

CALM FROM WITHIN

ONLY THE BACK

OF MY EYES HAVE SECRETS

INFESTATION OF THE BRAIN

TONGUES NAILED

DOWN FOR SAFETY

AS I EAT ON

FRUIT ONCE SWEET AND RIPE

THE APPLE OF

MY EYE

Turn on down to wonder
street

Green tiles make the front

On the corner

A pawner

Looking for your jewels

Not there now

Same goes for

The fools

Turn down to wonder
street

Olden day faces

Where you could

See them meet

Old navigation demolished

Man that's a shame

Turn down to wonder
street

That's what my old

Family told me

Turn down to wonder
street

Try see

HEART BEAT NO
LONGER

DEATHS CYCLE ARCS
STRONGER

ALL EMOTIONS LIE
DORMANT

FATE NEVER FORETOLD
TORMENT

I'm nothing like your other dreams

A simple sentence screams

I'm nothing like that hit man poet

With pencils and pens he just doesn't know
it

I'm inside somewhere deep n dreary

Loom large sounds I'm sure you hear me

Inside this moralistic temple

I will sit and sharpen all your wisdom

To stab n stare n grab at paper

To imitate is no longer in favour

You couldn't dream this simple sound

Of poetic prose getting laid right down

It's inside somewhere deep and delicious

To hear it man it can cut quite vicious

In a certain solid scheming way

As another poem coming your way

In the darkened room

Where I feel for sleep

Oh why did I not write down all my sheets

For certain nights

No poetic treats

For inside every melting man

Lies the visions within reach to

Spell out your dealt hand

Inside where the nail is now driven in

A coffin that peels and fades away

And on your grave stone where it stops

Vast poetic piece of prose

Chiselled hard for years for those

To come and weep and bring the flowers

To reads with pride

Of all your writing hours

Something sweet will be laid resting here

The bones of the poetic Man they fear.

I'm told to conform

In a poetic yawnnnnnn

I'm as sure and steady with this belief

Of fire in my belly

As brave as a titanic musician going down

Playing the tune

Of a sorrowful Neptune

Keeping firm and planted with thy feet.

I'm as sure and steady with this belief

Told I'm never up to scratch

In a wilderness of books that catch

Fire in a hail of publicity and hatch

Sequels that should be in the bin

Beginner stay real

Always hungry

Your time will begin

I won't fear you

Death

When you come

Black cloaked

Skeleton hand

I shall clasp

I know the flesh

Were done with that

Higher plains

A light

I'd never

Seen of this world

I thought I knew of

The full spectrum

Of colours

Yet this is something else

Like they merged now

All together into

A new colour

And you think and wait for some

Kind of scared feeling

But there's not

There's nothing but an

Emphatic feeling

Of moving on

Flying

Like when as human being

Watching birds soar

In awe thinking

Why can't I have wings?

Well you did

They were just

Enclosed within

And now they R spreading
out

Thick and heavy

Full of strength

And you will fly

Swift up to heaven

And begin

Also available from Dale Brendan Hyde

THE INK RUN

A NOVEL VIGILANTE

OTISS is an abused child, physically & mentally tortured for years in the home by his sadistic parents. His Father STAN plots an elaborate alibi enabling him to set up the boy for the murder of his own Mother.

A trial of sorts, hanging on the basis of a defense of automatism (murder when sleepwalking) sees a detainment to the FABERON institution for the criminal insane.

In this cloudy pond, where the staff are every bit as dangerous & disturbed as the patients.

Young OTISS is placed on a wing funded as a trial by the Government which uses olden day methods from centuries past to cure madness.

Eventually released a decade later as an even more tortured soul, he sets up THE VILLAGE EYE pub as a front to his real nocturnal activities of being a VIGILANTE.

Warning beatings on the scum of the village soon becomes tiresome as he reaches new limits of retribution.

Still traumatized from youth, will he find the courage to finally confront STAN?

You can't truly escape your blood lines DNA as fatal mistakes see a familiar face from the INSTITUTION reveal that our main protagonist has not been the only one keeping the VIGIL & upping the ANTE.

Coming soon from Dale Brendan Hyde

STITCHED

A MISCARRIAGE OF JUSTICE INQUIRY

ONCE YOU'RE DEAD

THE TRUTH BECOMES SO MUCH CLEARER

Coming soon from Dale Brendan Hyde

THE DICE

WITH ONE FATAL ROLL, IT COULD BE YOU!

Four serial killers busy doing what they do best. Although one is now dead as a coffin nail. Executed & fried good by old sparky for his heinous crime spree that totalled out at fourteen victims.

Two more are active in the general Texas area, yet the police don't even have them on their radar. The body count is rapidly rising.

Then across the Atlantic pond is the fourth. Where a stop start investigation has come to a halt. Baffled, the Greater Manchester police can't decide if the mysterious pusher case is for real. Yet more bodies keep floating up from the canal areas and to one detective he's convinced that a serial killer is roaming the darkened towpaths looking for fresh victims.

In amongst all this mayhem is widower Shail Singleton. Ten years now she has lived in small town dripping springs, Texas. After fleeing her beloved Ireland with the still raw memory of her husband murdered on their own doorstep.

She only has one good trusted friend in this new town. Old Walter runs the local thrift shop and he understands her fears & dreams. Unbeknown to Shail though, all these lives are inextricably linked. And they are hurtling to a murderous conclusion, for even the executed leave things behind.